KU-213-204

Everyday Clothes

Schools Library and Infomation Services

Copyright © ticktock Entertainment Ltd 2006
First published in Great Britain in 2006 by ticktock Media Ltd.,
Unit 2, Orchard Business Centre, North Farm Road,
Tunbridge Wells, Kent, TN2 3XF
ISBN 1 86007 983 0 Pbk
Printed in China
A CIP catalogue record for this book is available from the British Library.

Picture credits
t=top, b=bottom, c=centre, l-left, r=right
Corbis: 16-17 all, 26r, 27r, 28r. Rex Features: 24bl, Werner Forman Archive: 2, 6b, 8-9 all, 10-11 all, 12-13 all, 20-21 all.

Every effort has been made to trace the copyright holders, and we apologise in advance for any unintentional omissions. We would be pleased to insert the appropriate acknowledgements in any subsequent edition of this publication.

- *Glossary terms are emboldened on first use on each spread*

Many animals, such as cats, groom their fur. Pigs smother themselves in mud; insects spin cocoons. But humans are the only creatures to create coverings for their bodies that can be removed, replaced and renewed.

Belonging

Clothes can show which tribe or nation we belong to. They may also reveal our gender, and whether we are married or single. Clothes can make a political statement, or proclaim our religion. They can give onlookers clues about the work we do, how much money we have, and the image we hope to create for ourselves.

What happened to very old everyday clothes?

They were recycled as rags or bandages

The skirt worn by this Masai woman from East Africa shows that she is married and belongs to a wealthy family.

More than useful

Clothes are useful; they shield our skin and protect us from scratches and bruises. They keep us warm and dry or cool and comfortable. They cheer us with bright colours, and pamper us with soft textures. More than this, clothes serve as signs of our identity. They send out messages about us, describing our place in the world.

Members of the same age group often choose similar clothes.

Traditional or modern?

Today, many different kinds of clothes are worn all round the world. Some, like an **abayah** or a hijab are traditional. They are based on ancient designs belonging to one particular group of people. Others, such as jeans and tee-shirts, have a much shorter history. They were created within the past hundred years, and can only be made by modern machines.

This young woman is wearing a modern version of traditional Muslim hijab (modest dress).

Clothes for everyday

In the past, most ordinary people could only afford one set of clothes at a time. They wore them everyday. Compared with elaborate fashions,

A pair of working class late 1890's winter boots.

worn only by rich people, everyday clothes were practical and long lasting. Their designs changed very slowly. Most were worn - and mended - year after year, until they finally fell to pieces.

THE FIRST EVERYDAY CLOTHES

No-one knows exactly when the first clothes were made. But many historians think clothing was invented some time between 50,000 BC – 100,000 BC. This was the time when modern humans (homo sapiens) left their warm homeland in Africa and migrated to live in colder parts of the world.

Furs and hides

The first clothes were made from the furs or **hides** (skins) of large wild animals. They were preserved by rubbing with fat or hanging over a cool, smoky fire. After around 30,000 BC, clothes-makers used stone knives to trim skins and needles of bone or mammoth-ivory to sew them together.

Furs and skins were sewn by pushing a needle through holes made by a sharp-pointed blade.

Tunics, trousers, trimmings

The first sewn garments were sleeveless tunics, worn by men or women. They were made from two cut and shaped animal skins, stitched together at the shoulders. Wearers either went bare legged, or wrapped their feet and legs with strips of animal skin. Trousers were invented later - between 20,000 BC – 10,000 BC.

Sioux Chief's War Leggings dating from the end of the 18th century.

The earliest woven garments were sheep's wool blankets. They looked similar to the traditional blankets worn by Masai men in Africa today.

Squeezing and weaving

Early people also created clothes by processing natural fibres. They twisted tall plant stems into string, and hammered tree-bark to make fabric. They produced felt by boiling and squeezing animal hair, and spun thread by twirling plant fibres or sheep's wool. At first, string and thread were only used for nets, bags and braids. But later thread was woven into cloth, on wooden frames called looms.

Silk and cotton

What were skins and furs sewn together with?

Animal sinews (bands of stretchy flesh that attach muscles to bones) or lengths of hair from animals and tails.

Around 3000 BC, people living in India and China found ways of creating finer, more delicate fibres. Chinese workers unwound miles of natural silk thread from **cocoons** made by silk-moth grubs, and wove it into shimmering **gauze** (thin, transparent fabric). At the same time, Indus Valley farmers harvested fluffy cotton wool (the fibre around cotton-seeds), spun it into thread then wove into light, cool cloth.

Indian saris – long lengths of fabric, carefully folded at the waist and draped round the body – were some of the earliest clothes to be made from cotton cloth, and later in silk (right).

7

T he climate of Egypt, in North Africa, is hot and very dry. Because of this, the Ancient Egyptians wore very few clothes. However, they were some of the earliest men and women to wear clothing made from woven fabric, rather than animal skins and furs.

What was the Egyptians' favourite fabric?

Crisp, cool, white linen. The Egyptians believed the gods wore it in heaven.

Wall Painting of Ramses III wearing an elaborate loincloth.

Simple shapes

Egyptian clothes were simple – just lengths of fabric, folded into convenient shapes then pinned or tied around the body. For working in their fields, Egyptian men wore brief **loincloths** (strips of fabric wrapped between the legs like a nappy/diaper) or short lengths of fabric wound around the waist, like kilts (wrapped skirts). Both styles were held in place by knotting two ends of the garment together, or by belts made of leather or rope.

Unchanging styles

Women's clothes were made of a larger piece of cloth, wrapped right around the body from the breast to the ankle. Sometimes, two small pieces were used instead, and stitched together at the sides. Both methods created a long, narrow, tube-shaped garment, which was stopped from slipping down by two wide shoulder straps. It stayed in style for almost 2,000 years.

A straight, simple, narrow dress was everyday wear for most Egyptian women. Natural cream and white (for linen) and fawn or grey (for wool) were the usual shades.

Sleeves and pleats

After around 1530 BC, invaders from West Asia introduced new clothing designs. Egyptian men and women began to wear extra lengths of fabric draped loosely over their arms and shoulders. These created wide, baggy sleeves, and were held in place, front and back, by tight waist belts or metal pins. Men also began to wear double-layer kilts with extra front and side panels. Pleated clothes draped gracefully, trapped cool air close to the body, and let the wearer move freely.

The Egyptian man on the left wears a kilt with a wide, pleated front panel. The man on the right wears a simpler, old-style kilt, tied at the waist.

Furs and fringes

At night, when desert temperatures fell quickly, Egyptian men and women wrapped themselves warm blankets, woven from sheep's wool. But their neighbours in colder, mountainous lands of West Asia continued to wear thick, bulky cloaks of sheepskin and fur. These Asians also wove woollen cloth decorated with fringes and tassels to look like shaggy animal skins.

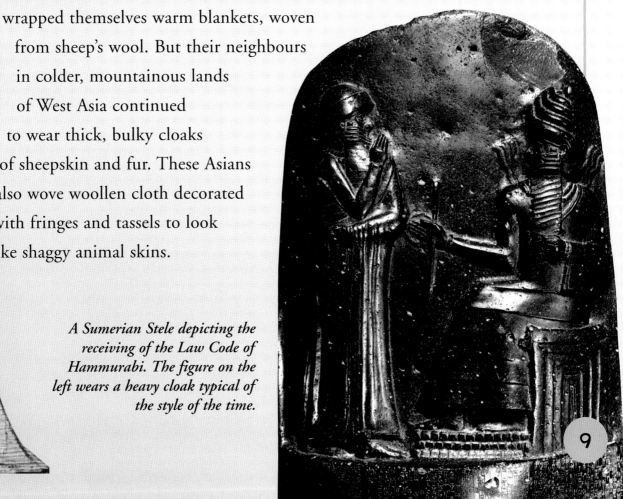

A Sumerian Stele depicting the receiving of the Law Code of Hammurabi. The figure on the left wears a heavy cloak typical of the style of the time.

9

Greek traders travelled throughout the Mediterranean region, making contact with peoples in Europe, Africa and West Asia and picking up clothing fashions along the way. Greek clothes were made of Greek sheep's wool, Turkish linen, and silk imported from China.

Minoan style

The earliest Greek civilisation developed around 0000 BC on the island of Crete. Its rulers were rich and extremely powerful. Wall-paintings record clothes worn by ordinary people, as well as by noblemen and women. Cretan people had few garments, but their clothes were brightly coloured and often decorated with embroidered designs. Men wore **loincloths** of wool, leather or linen, fastened by tight belts. Women wore full, **flounced** skirts and close-fitting jackets, which sometimes left the breasts uncovered.

Cloaks and tunics

On the Greek mainland, the everyday dress for men was a knee-length **chiton** (tunic), made of woollen fabric seamed or pinned at the shoulders and the sides. In cold weather, a **chamlys** (short cloak) or **himation** (long cloak) was worn on top. Old men, and men in authority, often wore long tunics that reached to the ground.

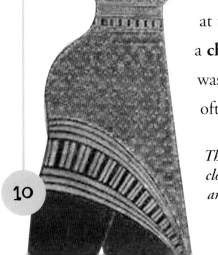

This young Cretan serving man is wearing a close-fitting loincloth with a fish-scale pattern and a wide decorative border.

The woman wears a long, flowing peplos. Like many Greek children, her son is naked, except for a chiton (short cloak) around his shoulders.

Graceful and comfortable

Greek women's clothes were made in a similar way to men's, from long, unstructured, lengths of cloth. The most common women's garment was the **peplos**, made by pinning a length of cloth at the shoulders, then binding it close to the body by a **girdle** (band of braid or ribbon) tied round the waist and below the breasts. Outside the home, Greek women wore a himation (cloak) as well, and used part of it to veil their heads and faces.

How did Greeks make clothes to fit each wearer?

By weaving each length of cloth specially for the person who would wear it.

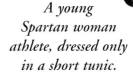

A young Spartan woman athlete, dressed only in a short tunic.

Greek farmers dressed in the traditional himation *and* chamlys.

Uncovered

Greek men often went naked – especially when working in a hot environment. A fit and healthy body was admirable, and likely to be the home of a good or noble soul. In contrast, respectable Greek women wore long clothes that covered most of their bodies. But the city-state of Sparta was famous for the freedom given to its women – and for the short, man-like clothes they wore.

THE ROMAN EMPIRE

The Romans' home in central Italy was close to Ancient Greek lands. Like Greek clothes, early Roman garments were just lengths of fabric, folded to fit the body. But towards the end of the Roman era, clothes styles began to change, as the Romans learned new designs and techniques from peoples they ruled.

The toga

The earliest Roman garment was the toga. Originally, it was the only piece of clothing Roman men and women wore, but by around 200 BC, it had become a sign of Roman citizenship, and was restricted to men only. Each **toga** was a huge, heavy woollen cloak, shaped like a half circle. It was made by trimming away the lower corners from a long rectangle of cloth.

"Barberini Man Wearing a Toga", carrying busts of two ancestors Centrale Montemartini, Capitoline Museums

Ready for work

A long, heavy toga made it difficult for the wearer to move quickly or do hard physical work. So, from around 200 BC, most ordinary Roman men – and slaves - wore short tunics, similar to the Greek **chiton**. Underneath, they wore a **loincloth**; on top, when it was cold, they wore a blanket or a short, hooded cloak.

A Roman soldier dressed in a short tunic, ideal for easy movement.

The layered look

Roman women also wore tunics, but floor-length, draped, and tied with decorative **girdles**. Often, they wore two or more tunics at the same time. (Eventually, the outer tunic became known as a **stola**.) Over their tunics, women wore a long cloak, called a **palla**, and, sometimes, a veil. Women's underwear included a lightweight loincloth and a supportive band of cloth around the breasts, called a **mammilare**.

Women's tunics were pinned at the shoulder and tied round the waist.

'Barbarian' clothes

At its peak, the Roman empire stretched from Scotland to Syria. 'Barbarian' (non-Roman) peoples living in conquered lands wore many different styles of clothing. Some were made from draped lengths of fabric, like the Romans' own. But others, such as trousers, were cut from woven fabric in shaped, separate sections, then carefully stitched together. After around AD 100, the Romans slowly began to copy them.

How big was a Roman toga?

On average, about 18 ft along its straight edge, and 5 ft 6 in at its widest point.

Trousers worn by a Celtic warrior dating from 500 BC. They were popular in north-west Europe, and with Central Asian nomad tribes.

MEDIEVAL EUROPE

At the start of the Middle Ages, people in southern Europe wore clothes similar to old Roman ones. But slowly, new ways of making clothes were invented. These created dramatically different new styles.

Typical tunics

In Europe, a T-shaped tunic remained the standard male garment. It was cut and sewn in a neater, less bulky shape than in previous centuries. It now had long sleeves, for warmth, belted round the waist, and worn with a thick cloak. In northern Europe, men also wore baggy trousers.

This 11th century illustration shows a wineseller dressed in a typical tunic of the time.

Surcoats and wimples

Early medieval women wore long, loose tunic-shaped dresses, sewn with side seams, and with long wide sleeves. Underneath, they wore a long **chemise** (loosely fitting dress), similar to men's. On top, they often wore a sleeveless **surcoat** (over-dress), cut and sewn in different regional designs, plus a heavy woollen cloak in winter weather. Married women covered their hair with scarves, veils or **wimples** (a wide band of cloth, hiding the neck and reaching up to the chin).

This Viking women, from around AD 1050, is wearing a long tunic topped by a two-piece overdress.

Fit and flare

By around AD 1300, craft workers in European cities had developed new tailoring skills. For the first time in Europe, men and women wore clothes with tight **bodices** (coverings for the top half of the torso) and separate, sewn-in sleeves. Men's tunics and women's dresses had flared skirts, with narrow waists and wide, sweeping hems.

*A woman servant in Italy, around AD 1350 wearing a dress with a tightly fitted bodice, flared skirt, low neckline and narrow, **tailored** sleeves.*

Dull colours

Everyday clothes, worn by ordinary people, began to be made in these new, fitted styles. But, unlike bright, patterned clothes, worn by the rich, they only appeared in plain colours. This was because ordinary people could not afford exotic imported fabrics, or expensive coloured dyes. Their everyday clothes were made from rough homespun wool or linen, in natural shades of cream, grey or brown or coloured with muted, earthy plant dyes.

A north-European family, around AD 1480, wearing stylishly shaped, but dull-coloured clothing.

What new invention did tight-fighting clothes require?

Adjustable fastenings - otherwise fitted styles would have been impossible to put on.

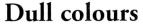

EASTERN REGIONS

Throughout most of Asia, ordinary people in the past worked out of doors as farmers, growing crops on the land, or tended flocks of sheep and cattle. Their everyday clothes had to protect them from extreme weather conditions.

Men from Algeria wore traditional robes to protect them from sunburn.

Loose and cool

In many parts of West Asia, men and women wore long, loose, flowing tunic, with wide sleeves. On top, they wore a robe which was given names such as **jubba**. They were simply made, from lengths of cloth stitched together without tailoring. Fabrics included cotton, linen and wool.

It's a wrap!

In India, ancient styles based on lengths of fabric wrapped around the body, continued to prove useful for thousands of years. Indian women folded and draped long lengths of cloth into graceful saris. There were many regional variations. Indian men wore a **dhoti**, a rectangle of cloth that could be wrapped like a skirt, or wound between the legs to create loose, baggy trousers. Similar styles developed in south-east Asia, where they were worn by men and women, and called **sarongs**.

Statues from a temple, carved around 1200. They show worshippers wearing long, wrapped dhotis.

Caftans and trousers

In northwest India, and neighbouring lands, everyday clothes developed from garments worn by the ancient Persians. The most important was the **caftan**, a fitted, long-sleeved coat, opening down the front, usually worn over trousers. Caftans became popular from Turkey to Mongolia. Persian-style baggy trousers also spread to north-west India (now Pakistan), where women wore them with long tunics. (Today, this combination is known as salwar kameez.)

How did Chinese workers keep warm in winter?

They wore jackets padded with cotton wadding.

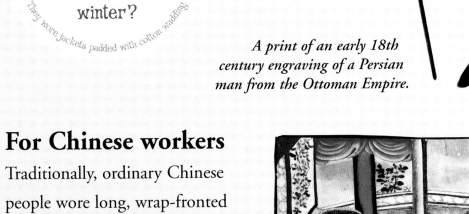

A print of an early 18th century engraving of a Persian man from the Ottoman Empire.

For Chinese workers

Traditionally, ordinary Chinese people wore long, wrap-fronted robes, or short, front-fastening jackets. Both styles tied with a sash around the waist, and were paired with long cotton or linen skirts or loose trousers. But when Manchu invaders from the north conquered China in 1644, they forced Chinese workers to wear clothes similar to Manchu styles. These included long, loose robes with wide sleeves and high collars.

Chinese tea-packers, painted around AD 1750. They are wearing traditional Chinese jackets, wide trousers and sashes.

17

AFRICA

In most of Africa, the climate was warm all year round. The land was covered with dense rainforest, or tall grasses and thorn bushes. Most men and women led very active lives, and tight, complicated clothes would have stopped them from travelling far, or working. Children often went naked for the first few years of life.

Bark and leather

The earliest African clothes were made of natural substances. For example, in southern and east-central Africa, leather from hunted animals, or specially treated tree-bark, was made into aprons. These were worn in pairs, at the front and the back of the body, by men and unmarried girls. Married women a leather skirt and cloak, instead.

Leather garments were often decorated with fringes, strips of animal fur, or beads.

Wrapped cloth

The first woven cloth in Africa was made around 3000 BC. Over the centuries, African weavers became very skilful at spinning thread from wool, goat hair, or plant fibres such as raffia, dying it in brilliant colours, and weaving it into cloth. They also obtained rough silk thread by unwrapping African moth **cocoons**. Most garments were not cut or sewn, but just draped and tied around the body. Wrapped styles included simple blanket-cloaks, worn by East African cattle-herders, and pure white wrap-around robes, worn in Ethiopia.

East-African cloak. Fastened at the shoulder, it leaves both hands free for work.

Robes and slings

In crop-growing and trading communities, especially in West Africa, wrapped clothes became more elaborate as individual wealth increased and people could afford more fabric. Successful men wore full wrap-around robes draped in impressive, dignified styles. New designs for men appeared, such as the tunic made from a length

A Nigerian wearing a traditional expansive tunic.

What was Aso Adire?

Dyed cloth, made in West Africa and used for everyday clothes.

of folded cloth with an opening for the head. West African women wore long wrapped skirts or full-length wrap dresses. They also wound lengths of cloth around their backs to carry young babies in.

Modest and practical

In North Africa, harsh desert conditions made nakedness uncomfortable. Long robes, for men and women, were cooler and more airy. After around AD 700, a new religion made covering the body essential for most North African people. They converted to Islam, which teaches that men and women should both be modestly dressed. Muslim soldiers from Asia also brought new styles with them, especially trousers. These became everyday wear under long, loose robes, for many North African men. North African women also wore long robes, topped by cloaks and wide, **gauzy** scarves or veils.

North African robes were made from a long length of fabric, folded in two, and left partly open on either side of the body. The openings served as sleeves, and provided coolness.

19

THE AMERICAS

Early humans first reached Alaska, in the far north of America, some time before 35,000 BC. Slowly, they spread southwards, reaching tip of South America by around 9000 BC. Different groups settled in separate localities, and developed their own styles of clothing for everyday wear.

Soft warm fleece

American clothes were made from materials that were available locally. These varied widely from place to place. Some were found only in America. In the high Andes Mountains region, Inca women wove **ponchos** (thick cloaks like blankets, with a hole for the head) from the soft, warm fleece of native llama and alpaca, dyed in vivid colours. Ponchos were worn by men over knee-length tunics, woven from plant fibres. Inca women wore loose, straight-sided ankle-length dresses.

The Incas mummified dead bodies. They wrapped them in woven blankets and ponchos.

Pelts and furs

In icy Arctic regions of North America, Inuit and Aleut peoples made clothes from the skins of animals they hunted for food: deer, caribou, polar bears, seals and foxes. These all had thick, shaggy, waterproof coats, that had evolved to help them survive in bitter weather. Arctic men

Which goods brought by Europeans replaced quills as decoration for clothes?

Brightly coloured glass beads.

and women all wore similar garments: a hooded tunic, called a **parka** or **anorak**, trousers and boots. In winter, they added extra tunics, called kuletak.

Skins, tails and paws

Other Native North Americans, also made clothes from animal skins. After cleaning them and softening them they sewed them together to make tunics for men or long dresses for women. At first, clothes-makers left the animals' manes, tails or paws in position as decoration. Later, they cut the skins to shape, and added colourful trimmings such as brightly-dyed porcupine quills.

This European portrait of an Inuit man from Alaska shows him dressed from head to toe in fur-lined clothes.

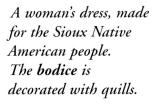

*A woman's dress, made for the Sioux Native American people. The **bodice** is decorated with quills.*

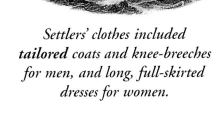

*Settlers' clothes included **tailored** coats and knee-breeches for men, and long, full-skirted dresses for women.*

Settler styles

When the first Europeans arrived to settle in America, they brought clothes styles from their homelands with them. But their life in the 'New World' was harsh; many also disapproved of finery, for religious reasons. So they wore tough, hardwearing clothes, in dark, sober colours, made from extra-thick cloth and leather.

EUROPE 1500~1750

After around 1500, clothing styles began to change more quickly. Clothes were very expensive, however, so people chose new garments for their hard-wearing qualities, as well as for their appearance. A new outfit was expected to last for at least 10 years.

Rich and poor

Wealthy people followed the latest fashions. In the 16th century, these featured tight corsets, stiffened skirts, **trunk-hose** (baggy shorts, fastened tightly round the thigh) and padded **doublets** (jackets). Ordinary peoples' clothes reflected fashionable shapes, but were looser and lighter. Men wore simple knee-length breeches, and women's skirts ended above the ankle.

This fashionable silk dress, was worn by a wealthy noblewoman around 1740.

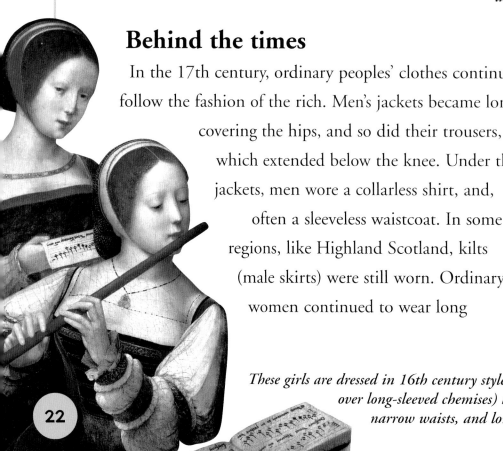

Behind the times

In the 17th century, ordinary peoples' clothes continued to follow the fashion of the rich. Men's jackets became longer, covering the hips, and so did their trousers, which extended below the knee. Under their jackets, men wore a collarless shirt, and, often a sleeveless waistcoat. In some regions, like Highland Scotland, kilts (male skirts) were still worn. Ordinary women continued to wear long

These girls are dressed in 16th century style. Their dresses (worn over long-sleeved chemises) have low square necks, narrow waists, and long, full skirts.

Which country was considered the most fashionable at this time?

France.

dresses with close-fitting **bodices**. Underneath, they wore a **chemise** and petticoats. For extra warmth, men and women wore cloaks; women also wore shawls and kerchiefs.

In 17th century Britain, fashionable royal courtiers wore clothes trimmed with ribbons, lace and bows. Ordinary people wore plainer styles.

Revolutionary styles

Everyday clothes carried a political message, especially in 18th century France. Poor people, who often went hungry, were outraged to see the extravagant clothes worn by wealthy nobles. In return, rich politicians criticised the poor for being dressed in rags.

French protesters, dressed in ordinary, everyday clothes, were nicknamed '**sans-culottes**'. They did not wear – and could not afford – the fashionable, **tailored** knee-breeches (culottes).

This early printed picture shows protesters attacking nobles in knee-breeches (left) and two poor people (far right) in ragged everyday clothes.

Homespun clothes

Ordinary men and women could not afford fashionable materials, such as lace, muslin (fine cotton), silk and velvet; they wore linen, hemp and wool. Often, cloth was woven from thread spun from local sheep's fleece by ordinary women, in their homes. They sold it to travelling merchants, who re-sold it to weavers in towns.

New inventions transformed everyday clothing after around 1750. Sewing machines meant that clothes could be stitched together much more quickly than before. Railways and cheap newspapers spread details of the latest fashions to ordinary people throughout Europe and the USA.

When were sewing machines invented?

Chain-stitch machines were invented in 1856, lock-stitch machines in 1860

Cotton for all

Originally, cotton was a rare, precious cloth, imported to Europe from India. But by the mid 19th century, new steamships carried vast quantities of raw cotton to European factories, where it was spun, woven and sewn on machines to make cheap clothing for everyday. In the USA, cotton was grown on southern plantations worked by slaves, then sent to northern cities for processing.

This replica cotton dress, made of costly fabric, would have been worn by a fashionwealthy woman around 1810.

Workwear and underwear

Cotton clothes soon became popular for among working families. Cotton was much easier to wash than old-style wool, and far quicker to dry. Machine-made cotton garments were cheap, too.

Cotton absorbed sweat and was cool and comfortable – especially in hot working environments, such as iron foundries and factories.

*This 19th-century farmworker is wearing a long-sleeved **chemise**, fitted **bodice** and full skirt.*

Cotton was used to make tough clothes for male workers, such as full-length trousers and aprons, and also for men's shirts and underpants. For women, cotton cloth was sewn into blouses, camisoles (sleeveless tops, worn next to the skin), aprons, petticoats – and knickers.

Country traditions

Before sewing machines were invented, cotton clothes were sewn by hand, usually in women's homes. In the countryside, working people continued to make many of their own everyday clothes by hand, using traditional materials and following traditional styles. But increasingly, they travelled to towns, to buy machine-made clothing there.

Fashion for all

By around 1900, cheap, machine-made garments, together with fashion magazines brought the latest styles closer to ordinary people. Women, especially, became much more fashion-conscious. They wanted their everyday clothes to look up-to-date, yet still be practical to wear. So they looked for fashion details, such as high 'choker' necklines, when buying a sensible new outfit, or added fashionable trimmings, such as braid and lace, to existing everyday clothes.

This picture from a fashion magazine shows the latest styles of for women's coats (left) and dresses (right) around AD 1900.

In the early 20th century, new technology, continued to increase the range of cheap, mass-produced everyday clothes for ordinary people to wear. Clothing styles still followed high fashion, but were also influenced by social changes, economic crises, and two World Wars.

Washing clothes at an Italian street fountain, 1907. The women wear aprons and shawls over their dresses. The boy wears trousers and a knitted sweater.

Regional variations

In poor regions such as southern Europe, women wore dresses with tight **bodices** and long skirts. Men wore long, straight trousers, with shirts and jackets or waistcoats. Around the coast, fishermen and sailors preferred hand-knitted woollen sweaters. In the American West, farmhands and cowboys dressed in shirts and narrow jeans trousers made of tough blue denim. The design had been patented by Levi Strauss in the 1870s.

Wartime and 'Flappers'

During World War I (1914-1918), millions of men were in uniform. Off duty, they wore clothes similar to late 19th century peacetime styles. These included three-piece suits, worn by clerks in offices, and woollen jackets with thick trousers, for country

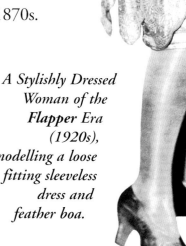

A Stylishly Dressed Woman of the Flapper Era (1920s), modelling a loose fitting sleeveless dress and feather boa.

workers. However, women's clothes changed dramatically, as they took over fighting men's jobs - driving trains, fighting fires and making weapons. For ease of movement, and for safety, they took off their stiff, wasp-waisted corsets and cut their skirts short (around 8 inches off the ground).

America labourers pictured in the 1920s in more casual clothing.

Work and leisure

What were jeans originally called?

'Waist overalls'

In the 1920s and 1930s, male labourers working in factories, at construction sites, and on farms, wore all-in-one heavy cotton overalls. Men employed in shops and offices dressed in neat suits and ties. But for leisure wear, most men chose similar styles: relaxed, baggy trousers and a loose jacket or knitted sweater. Zip fasteners, mass–produced from the 1930s, replaced buttons and buckles for leisure wear.

Uniform styles

Women's dresses in the 1930s became slightly longer, and more fitted, as a reaction to the 1920s boyish styles. In 1939, World War II began. Large numbers of women volunteered to join the armed forces, and, even off duty, their everyday clothes were based on sensible, masculine, uniform styles. Skirts were the shortest yet (knee length), with crisp pleats. Frocks had collars like battledress; jackets were short and square-shouldered, like men's.

A wartime costume (jacket and skirt) and dress, 1940. Legs were often bare, since silk and fine cotton, used for knitted stockings, were in very short supply.

27

20TH CENTURY 1950-2000

In the second half of the 20th century, all kinds of clothing, from everyday garments to high-fashion designs, changed more quickly than ever before. Ideas about wearing clothes changed, as well. There were fewer rules about 'correct' or 'suitable' dressing.

Utility styles for all the family in the early 1950s.

Utility

Many countries in Europe were devastated by World War II. Clothing was scarce, and hard to buy, and many governments rationed fibres and fabrics even after the war and added high taxes to luxury imports. They also encouraged citizens to not to throw old, worn clothes away. Men's suits and women's dresses were plain and simple, used no unnecessary fabric , and were often patched or darned.

Made in the USA

In the 1940s and 1950s, the USA was the world leader in popular entertainment. Blue jeans, seen in cowboy movies, began to be sold beyond Western states in the 1950s. American knitted cotton sportswear, such polo-necks and tee-shirts, replaced shirts made of **broadcloth** (woven fabric) for informal, everyday occasions. Comfortable but form-fitting knitted cotton briefs were favourite male and female underwear. By the 1960s, new, artificial fibres, such as nylon (invented by US **chemists**) were used for everyday clothes.

Marlon Brando in A Streetcar Named Desire in jeans and t-shirt.

Anything goes

The 1960s were a time of social experiment and political discontent. Young people rebelled against authority, and chose their own everyday clothes. These combined shapes, fabrics and decorations from many ethnic traditions with the latest high-fashion designs. For the first time, trends in everyday clothing were set by ordinary men and women, not by a rich, privileged elite. Although it provoked protests, women also began to wear trousers as ordinary, everyday clothes.

Which undergarment became popular because of mini-skirts?

Tights. Before the 1960s, most Western women wore stockings and suspenders.

The most famous 1960s garment was the mini-skirt, up to 6 inches above the knee, pioneered by 'alternative' British designer, Mary Quant.

Sportswear spin-off

Everyday wear based on comfortable sports clothes was first made by French designer Coco Chanel in the 1920s and 1930s. By the end of the 20th century, mass-produced versions of sports-style clothes, such as shells-suits (a type of tracksuit), joggers and sweatshirts, were the Western world's most popular everyday leisure wear. New elastic fibres, such as Lycra (TM), invented in the USA in 1959, were added to knitted or woven fabrics during manufacture. They allowed a much closer fit, fewer wrinkles and gave extra flexibility.

Sports-style clothes were first worn by young people, but were soon chosen by older men and women, as well.

GLOBAL STYLES TODAY

Today, Western media and Western-based corporations dominate world communications and world trade. Their power has helped spread Western social attitudes and visual styles all round the globe. Because of this, in many societies everyday clothes are now much less formal than before.

What material was added to jeans in the 1990s?

Lycra, to improve the fit.

Young peoples' everyday clothes include jeans, tee-shirts, hooded tops, and trainers.

Peer-group pressure

Following trends set in the 1960s, today's young people mostly like to wear similar styles. Wearing different clothes can lead to criticism or rejection by their **peers** (equals). In the same way, business men and women choose similar **tailored** suits for everyday office wear, worldwide. Other global everyday clothes are chosen for practicality. For example, labourers and engineers still wear overalls, though they are often made of artificial fibres rather than old-style cotton.

Maintaining tradition

In some parts of the world, people still prefer to wear traditional clothes everyday. This is the case in many Muslim countries, where

This Quechua woman is shown wearing traditional everyday clothing

religious beliefs encourage all men and women to be modestly and traditionally dressed. Alternatively, some Muslims may choose Western clothes for home, but cover them with a traditional robe when they go out of doors. In other regions, such as India, Africa and South America, traditional styles are still sometimes favoured, especially for important occasions. People there feel proud of past everyday clothing styles, even though they might not wear them all the time.

In recent years, companies and campaigners have worked together to end 'sweatshop' manufacturing such as this one in Mumbai.

Controversial

Today, international corporations build factories in developing countries where wages are low, and building costs are less expensive than Europe or the USA. This results in cheaper clothing, but many workers in developing countries are poorly-paid or exploited. Clothes-makers in developed countries often lose their jobs as a result. And governments quarrel over trade arrangements, trying to regulate imports and exports, and achieve a fair exchange.

International brands

In the same way, international clothing brands have caused comment and, sometimes, criticism – although they are also popular with consumers, and widely admired. Some politicians, artists and campaigners regret the disappearance of traditional garments as everyone chooses modern, global brands. Costume historians and folklore experts collect surviving examples of old-style everyday clothes, to study, record and preserve in museums.

By purchasing popular brands, customers decide what today's global everyday clothes shall be.

abayah Long, loose robe worn in Arab countries.

anorak Hooded, fur-lined tunic, worn by the Inuit people of the Eastern Arctic region.

bodice Garment (or part of a garment) covering the upper part of the body, from the shoulders to the waist.

broadcloth Cloth woven on a loom.

caftan Long coat, opening at the front. Originated in Persia (now Iran) worn by many Asian peoples.

chamlys Ancient Greek short cloak.

chemise Long tunic, made of fine woven fabric, worn as an undergarment from the Middle Ages until the 19th century.

chiton Ancient Greek short tunic.

cocoon Other casing, usually made of spun thread, made by insect grubs to protect themselves while they are transforming into adults.

dhoti Length of cloth, worn by Indian men. It could be wrapped round the body like a skirt or like baggy trousers.

djellaba Tunisian name for a long loose robe, worn as an outer garment in many North African and West Asian countries. See **jubba**.

doublet Tight fitting jacket, worn in Europe the 16th century.

drawers Long, loose underpants, worn originally by men and later also by women.

fashion plate Printed illustration in a an early women's magazine, designed to inform readers about new styles.

felt Thick cloth made of boiled, compressed wool or animal hair.

flappers Rebellious young women in 1920s Europe and the USA.

flounced With layers of frills.

girdle Decorative band (usually braid or ribbon) worn to fasten a garment around the waist.

hide The skin of cattle and other large animals, such as deer or buffalo.

himation Ancient Greek long cloak.

gauze Fine, transparent fabric, often woven from silk threads.

jubba Syrian name for a long loose robe, worn as an outer garment in many North African and West Asian countries. See **djellaba**.

loincloth Strip of baric wound around the hips and between the legs like a nappy/diaper.

mammilare Band of fabric worn by women in Ancient Rome to cover and support.

palla Cloak worn by women in Ancient Rome.

parka Hooded, fur-lined tunic, worn by the Aleut people of the Western Arctic region. See **anorak**.

peers Social equals.

peplos Long robe worn by women in Ancient Greece. Made of a length of cloth wound round the body and folded over at the top, to create a double layer of fabric covering the upper torso.

poncho South American cloak, like a blanket with a hold for the head.

sans-culottes Nickname for political revolutionaries in 18th century France. They wore baggy trousers or kilts of rough linen; wealthy nobles wore tailored culottes (knee-breeches).

sarong Length of wide cloth wrapped around the body. Worn in many parts of South-East Asia.

sinews Bands of stretchy flesh that attach muscles to bones.

stola Outer tunic worn by women in Ancient Rome.

surcoat Over-dress (for women) over-tunic (for men)

tailored Cut and sewn to fit the shape of the body.

toga Cloak shaped like a half-circle, worn in Ancient Rome.

trunk hose Short, thigh-length trousers, fastened at the bottom to create a pouched or puffed effect, worn in 16th century Europe.

utility Usefulness. A style of clothing worn in Europe during and immediately after World War II.

wimple Band of cloth covering the neck from ear to ear, and from the collar-bone to the chin. Worn by women in Medieval Europe.